Wright Brothers
National Memorial
by Omega G. East

Division of Publications
National Park Service
U.S. Department of the Interior
Washington, D.C., 1961 (Reprint 1991)

> *The National Park System, of which Wright Brothers National Memorial is a unit, is dedicated to conserving the scenic, scientific, and historic heritage of the United States for the benefit and inspiration of its people.*

The National Park Service gratefully acknowledges the assistance of Dr. Marvin W. McFarland, who reviewed the manuscript and gave many valuable suggestions. We are grateful also for the excellent contemporary photographs made available by the Library of Congress. All photographs used in this book, except those otherwise credited, were furnished by the Library of Congress.

Aircraft over the Wright memorial shaft depict a half century of aviation history. *Courtesy, North Carolina Department of Conservation and Development, Raleigh, N.C.*

Wright Brothers

National Memorial – North Carolina

By Omega G. East

Digital Reprint of:

National Park Service Historical Handbook Series No.34

Please inquire with the Park Service directly about any tour map changes.

Digital Scanning and Publishing is a leader in the electronic republication of historical books and documents. We publish many of our titles as eBooks, paperback and hardcover editions. DSI is committed to bringing many traditional and well-known books back to life, retaining the look and feel of the original work.

Trade Paperback ISBN: 978-1-58218-887-4

All rights reserved, which include the right to reproduce this book or portions thereof in any form except provided by U.S Copyright Laws.

First DSI Printing: 2017
Digital Scanning, Inc. Scituate, MA 02066.
WWW.DigitalScanning.com
email: Info@digitalscanning.com

Contents

	Page
The Wright Brothers of Dayton, Ohio	1
Young Business Partners	3
Pioneers of Flight	5
Problems of Flight	9
First Experiments, 1899	10
Why Kitty Hawk?	13
Glider Experiments, 1900	14
Glider Experiments, 1901	19
Wind-Tunnel Tests, 1901	27
Glider Experiments, 1902	28
The Motor and the Propellers	33
The Powered Machine, 1903	36
December 17, 1903: The Day Man First Flew	44
After the First Flight	53
The Original Airplane Exhibited	60
The National Memorial	60
Guide to the Area	60
Administration	63
Glossary	63
Suggestions for Further Reading	64

KITTY HAWK AND KILL DEVIL HILLS are American place names that will live in history. Here Wilbur and Orville Wright, two unassuming brothers with a passion for advancing aeronautical knowledge, and the willingness to undertake a scientific adventure, made the world's first successful flight of a man-carrying, power-driven, heavier-than-air machine.

December 17, 1903, was the day man first flew in this machine. It was a cold and windy day when Orville Wright climbed aboard their plane at 10:35 a.m. His first power-driven flight of 120 feet lasted just 12 seconds when he flew over a wind-swept stretch of level sand now preserved at Wright Brothers National Memorial. From those moments the science of aeronautics has borne the impress of the Wrights' achievements.

The Wright Brothers of Dayton, Ohio

The two young men who were to be the first to fly were born in the midwest shortly after the Civil War. Wilbur Wright was born on a farm near Millville, 8 miles east of New Castle, Ind., April 16, 1867. Four years younger, Orville Wright was born in Dayton, Ohio, August 19, 1871. They were the sons of Rev. Milton Wright,

Wilbur Wright, about 1880.   Orville Wright, about 1880.

a minister, and later bishop, of the United Brethren Church, and Susan Koerner Wright. Both parents had been teachers. When his sons were small, Bishop Wright was editor of the church's publications. Mrs. Wright had "a streak of her father's mechanical ability," and she had a reputation in the family for being able "to mend anything." Bishop and Mrs. Wright also had two older sons, Reuchlin and Lorin, and a younger daughter, Katharine.

In the Wright home, children were encouraged to pursue intellectual interests and to investigate whatever aroused their curiosity. Wilbur and Orville displayed mechanical aptitude, the gift of original thinking, and a pioneering urge. Sharing a common interest in mechanical devices, the boys made kites and toy helicopters, built a lathe and a printing press that worked. Wilbur wrote of their close associations:

> From the time we were little children my brother Orville and myself lived together, played together, worked together and, in fact, thought together. We usually owned all our toys in common, talked over our thoughts and aspirations so that nearly everything that was done in our lives has been the result of conversations, suggestions and discussions between us.

Mrs. Wright died in 1889. It was that year that the brothers assembled their printing press from old parts found in junk yards and barns and began to publish a successful neighborhood weekly newspaper. Although each brother attended high school the full time required for a diploma, neither of them formally graduated from high school or attended college. Their two older brothers married and established homes of their own, but Wilbur and Orville remained bachelors. After completing their schooling they continued to live with their father and schoolteacher sister in a modest framehouse in Dayton.

The Wright home, 7 Hawthorne Street, Dayton, about 1897, three years before the first Kitty Hawk experiments. The house where Orville was born in 1871, and where Wilbur died in 1912.

West Side News.

Vol. 1. DAYTON, OHIO, MAY 25, 1889. No. 12

West Side News.

PUBLISHED WEEKLY.

Wilbur Wright · · · Editor
Orville Wright · · Publisher

TERMS.—Quarter of year, twenty cents Six weeks, ten cents.

1210 WEST THIRD STREET.
DAYTON, OHIO.

Ancient Warriors.

Before the invention of gunpowder a battle was little better than a group of hand-to-hand conflicts. Stout sinews and muscles were then valued, and the strong man was especially esteemed. William Wallace was the Scottish chief, not only for his patriotism but also because he had a giant's strength. Once, when attacked by five men, he killed thr— and put ...ght ... ...ough

Parrot Chorus.

The traditional "fish story" has many varieties, to which it seems only fair to add the following, even though the fish in this case was a parrot. Doubtless its narrator, an American artist, designed it to be "taken for what it is worth."

He was very fond of knocking about in out-of-the-way quarters of the world, and once left ship with a ship of comrades, in order to explore a Central American wilderness. During the cruise of several months, the entire ship's company had devoted their leisure hours to singing to a parrot. The sailor had also lost no opportunity of teaching the bird all the nautrical phrases they knew.

When the artist and his comrades had bidden the bird and the sailors good-by, they plunged into the heart of the tropical forest, and aft--- ---eat exertion in accomplish---

forsaking all others, cleave only unto her, so long as you both shall live!"

The minister paused for the response. The groom hung down his head, and was silent, but the bride, in a staccato tone, exclaimed, "Yes, sir, I'll see to it that he does all that?"

It was evident who would rule in that household. But a Scotch clergyman once married a groom who insisted upon promising to obey his wife. The clergyman, while traveling through a village, was requested to officiate at a marriage, in the absence of the parish minister. Just as he had told the bridegroom to love and honor his wife, the man interjected the words, "and obey." The clergyman, surprised to find a husband willing to take a promise usually made by the wife alone, did not heed the proposed amendment. He was going on with the ser---

---

The best, the cheapest and the safest place to buy a PIANO or ORGAN is at

Martin Bros. & Fritch,
W. Fourth St., Kuhns Block

Telephone 399.

JOHN M. NUTT
Attorney at Law,
Rooms 1 and 2 Kuhns Building

Remember that

APPLETON
will make your Photographs as cheap as any body, whether you have a ticket or not.

THE
WEST SIDF
Building ...

This successful neighborhood weekly was published by Orville Wright on a printing press assembled from old parts found in junkyards and barns. Wilbur Wright was editor. *Courtesy, Smithsonian Institution, Washington, D.C.*

Young Business Partners

Wilbur and Orville formed the Wright Cycle Company in 1892 to sell bicycles. Business increased, and they soon found that they needed to add a repair shop. Moderately successful, both in selling new bicycles and general repairing, the brothers twice moved their expanding business to larger quarters. As a next step they began to manufacture bicycles. They called their first bicycle the "Van Cleve" after their pioneer ancestors; a later model manufactured was named the "St. Clair"; and finally they made a low-priced model known as the "Wright Special." They manufactured several hundred bicycles of their own brand before discontinuing the business in order to devote their full time to aviation.

Inseparable companions in business and personal life, the brothers shared everything from a joint bank account to their laboratory work while unraveling the problems of flight. They were not longfaced and dour; both were sprightly and humor-loving. They loved small children and dogs, and they played musical instruments, sang, and enjoyed practical jokes.

3

Bishop Milton Wright, 1889. The father of Wilbur and Orville, Milton Wright (1828–1917) was a bishop in the Church of the United Brethren in Christ.

Katharine Wright, sister of Wilbur and Orville, about 1900.

Wright Cycle Company, 1127 West Third Street, Dayton. The left half of the brick building and the frame building in the rear were occupied by the Wrights.

Edwin H. Sines and Orville Wright in backroom of bicycle shop, 1897. Ed Sines was a boyhood friend of Orville Wright.

The bicycle business provided the funds for the Wrights' work in aviation, and afforded them sufficient leisure to pursue their interest in flying. Their father gave each of his children $1,000. This Wilbur and Orville invested in stock and never drew on for their aviation work—but it was there in case of necessity. They were never financed by anyone.

The repair and manufacture of bicycles sharpened the brothers' mechanical skill. The enterprise also developed their business experience, helpful later when they took the lead in founding the aviation industry. In their construction of flying machines, Wilbur and Orville often used the same equipment and tools used in repairing bicycles. They conducted many of their scientific experiments in the backroom of their shop, and most of the parts used in the first successful airplane were built there.

Pioneers of Flight

Since the dawn of history the idea of human flight has intrigued mankind. As the influence of the Wrights' achievements will last far into the future, so will the contributions of aeronautical pioneers

Lilienthal's two-surface glider of 1895 in which some of his highest and longest glides were made. This German engineer made hundreds of glides with various apparatuses employing birdlike wings.

who probed the mysteries of flight before Wilbur and Orville solved the problem. The research of these imaginative pioneer investigators influenced the brothers. In studying those earlier works the Wrights found many points that interested them. The knowledge that other pioneers had shared their faith in the possibility of heavier-than-air flight helped their morale.

In the pioneers' direct line of descent from the Greek legend of Daedalus and Icarius to the Wrights is Leonardo da Vinci. Da Vinci drew some interesting sketches in the late 15th century, though a machine built from his drawings could not possibly have flown. The interest in England of Sir George Cayley influenced other men to undertake the problem.

A Frenchman, Alphonse Pénaud experimented with toy helicopters, using twisted rubber bands for motive power. It was a Pénaud toy helicopter, given to Wilbur and Orville by their father, that first stirred their childhood interest in flying. However, in Europe, most experimenters had turned from heavier-than-air machines to lighter-than-air dirigible balloons by the time the brothers took up the problem of heavier-than-air flight. The American-born Sir Hiram Maxim, after spending $100,000, had abandoned his work; the machine built by Clément Ader, at the expense of the French Govern-

Otto Lilienthal (1848–96).

ment, had been a failure. None of the early experimenters attained sufficient knowledge of the aerodynamic principles involved to be able to design a successful powered machine capable of free, controlled, and sustained flight.

Only a few of the general public could distinguish between a heavier-than-air powered flying machine and a lighter-than-air gas bag equipped with propellers. Few knew that the problem of powered flight was not to fill a balloon with gas or hot air and float in it, or to glide in a complicated kite against air currents. Many among those who realized the obstacles to heavier-than-air flight in a powered machine believed it was as impossible as perpetual motion.

Wilbur and Orville acknowledged Otto Lilienthal, a famous German pioneer in aviation, as their greatest inspiration. Recognized as the father of gliding, Lilienthal made hundreds of glides with various apparatuses employing birdlike wings. First to explain scientifically why curved surfaces in a flying machine are superior to flat surfaces, Lilienthal's work on wing surfaces and air pressure proved valuable to the Wrights. Interested in scientific affairs, the brothers read with fascination and excitement, reports in 1895 of gliding flights by Lilienthal. But the art of gliding was neither a game nor child's play for aviation's pioneers. Lilienthal crashed and died as a result of a glider accident in 1896. Reading of his death, the Wrights wondered if they could go on from where he had left off.

Eventually the Wrights were ready to begin "a systematic study of the subject in preparation for practical work," and hoped to make contributions "to help on the future worker who will attain final

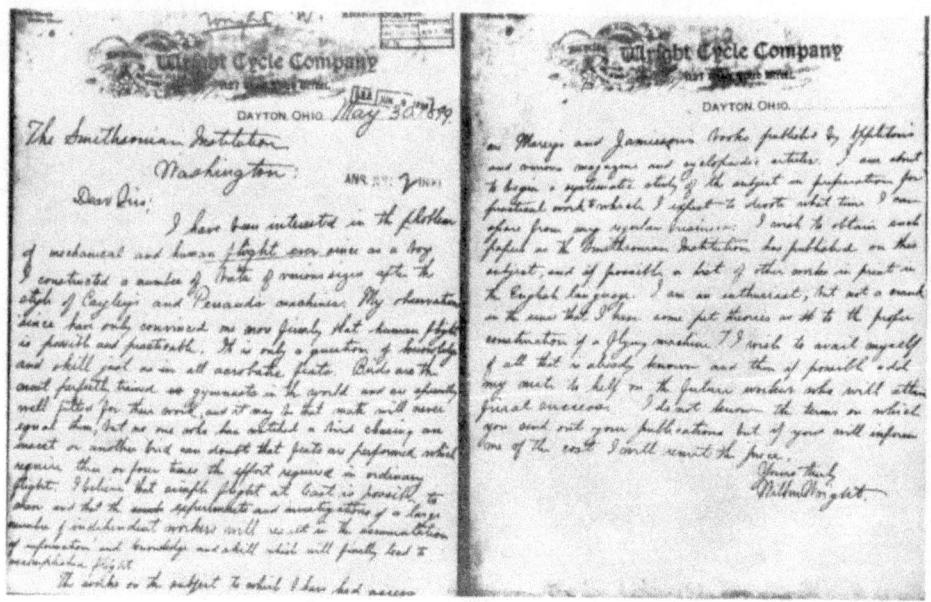

Courtesy, Smithsonian Institution.

success." Searching for, but finding little material on attempts to fly in the Dayton Public Library, Wilbur wrote, in May 1899, to the Smithsonian Institution in Washington seeking information about publications to read on aeronautics. The list of books and articles suggested by the Smithsonian included works by Dr. Samuel P.

Octave Chanute (1832–1910).

Samuel Pierpont Langley (1834–1906).

Langley who later became its director and secretary. The brothers were encouraged by seeing that a man of Langley's scientific standing believed in the possibility of flight at a time when few people did. Langley had been making aeronautical studies and experiments and succeeded in building power-driven models that flew. Later he built and attempted to fly a full-size, man-carrying powered machine; but in this he failed.

When a model flies, it does not necessarily follow that a full-size machine of the same design will also fly. As boys Wilbur and Orville had built model Pénaud helicopters that flew, but even the Wrights could not later have built a successful man-carrying machine by merely following Pénaud's same general design. The difficulty is—as early experimenters with model machines unhappily discovered—that when the linear measurement of a model is doubled it needs about eight times the power to make it fly.

Among the sources suggested by the Smithsonian was Octave Chanute's *Progress in Flying Machines*. Chanute, a successful contruction engineer living in Chicago, had directed experiments with gliders of his own design. A longtime encouraging friend and adviser to the Wrights, Chanute made an exhaustive study of the history of aeronautics.

Problems of Flight

A pioneer experimenter once said that "it is easy to invent a flying machine; it is more difficult to build one—but to make one fly is everything." As Lilienthal had seen, the Wrights also saw that, if ever they were to make progress in solving the problems of flight, they had not only to study them theoretically, but also to get up into the air in gliders and test their theories by actual practice. "If you are looking for perfect safety," said Wilbur, "you will do well to sit on a fence and watch the birds; but if you really wish to learn, you must mount a machine and become acquainted with its tricks by actual trial." Preferring the air to a fence, the brothers recognized that when undertaking to fly gliders their first major problem would be how to fly safely so they could live long enough to learn to fly a powered machine.

Wilbur wrote his father:

> I do not intend to take dangerous chances, both because I have no wish to get hurt and because a fall would stop my experimenting, which I would not like at all. The man who wishes to keep at the problem long enough to really learn anything positively must not take dangerous risks. Carelessness and overconfidence are usually more dangerous than deliberately accepted risks.

The problem of equilibrium was the second major problem that the brothers had to solve. They needed to devise measures to steer or control a flying machine both up and down and to each side.

When the Wrights started their investigations they believed that others had already solved the problems of how to design wings, propellers, and motors. Only later did they realize that they must also correctly design both the wings and the propellers and build their own motor. Thus their third major problem became how to design wings sufficiently strong to support the weight of the machine, motor, and pilot to take the greatest advantage of air particles providing lift by streaming along the upper and lower surfaces of the wings.

A fourth major problem that faced Wilbur and Orville was how to design a light-weight, high-powered engine and the propellers required to drive the machine through the air. They were to find that these problems were interrelated and that they would solve them only after 4½ years of spare-time study and experimentation.

First Experiments, 1899

Wilbur and Orville realized that the motion of the air on a flying machine is frequently variable and tricky, causing the machine to rear up or down, or one wing to rise higher than the other, and the machine to become unstable. The problem—how to control a flying machine—was to find a method of restoring the machine's equilibrium both up and down and to each side.

Most pre-Wright experimenters had relied on human control to balance flying machines. The operator simply shifted the weight of his body to tilt the wings in the direction opposite from adverse action of the wind. But the continual contortions and acrobatics required to maintain equilibrium by this method were not within the skill of many experimenters. While using it, both Lilienthal and Percy S. Pilcher, an English experimenter, were killed in nose dives.

Chanute sought to effect "automatic stability" independent of the operator by causing the flying machine's structurally automatic supporting surfaces to adjust positions by flexible joints automatically with changes in the wind. Wilbur and Orville were to conceive a different method of control than that sought by Chanute, though they themselves later designed and patented an "automatic" device—a pendulum analogous to Sperry's gyroscope.

At Dayton, in 1899, the Wrights were ready to move beyond the first phase of study, speculation, and discussion. Their combined attack on the problem of equilibrium resulted in the conception of one of the fundamental principles of aeronautics. Their reasoned

Data and calculations on pressures on an airfoil to achieve equilibrium in an airplane as worked out by the Wright Brothers in experiments in 1899.

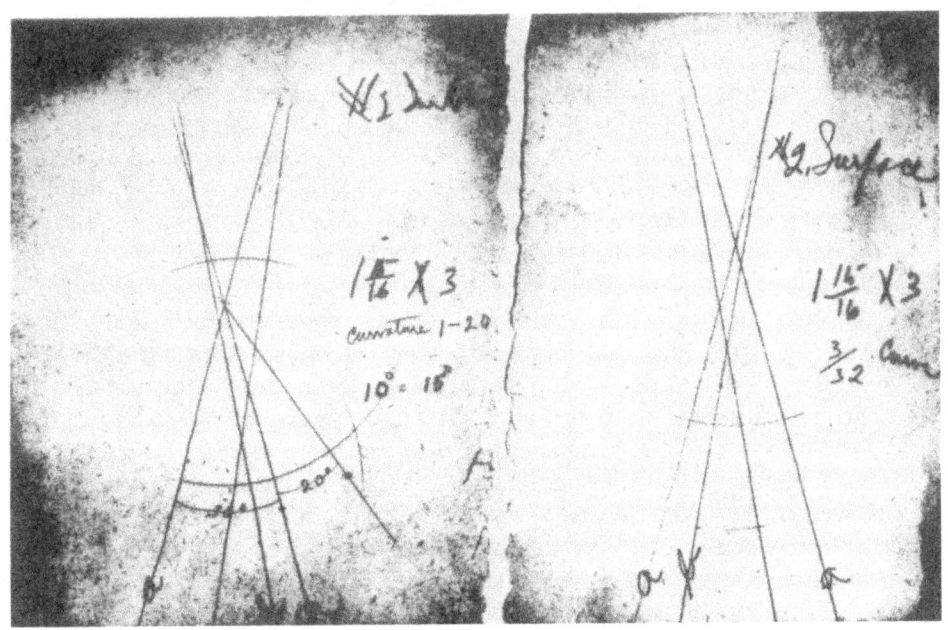

principle for lateral control of a flying machine was that the movement of an airfoil about its longitudinal axis could be controlled by means of a pressure differential exerted on its opposing lateral extremities (the principle known today as aileron control). Both modern-day ailerons and the Wrights' wing-warping are merely arbitrary mechanical devices for applying this principle. The brothers' first achievement was the conception of the principle itself.

Wilbur and Orville decided first to test their principle of control in a small model glider to see if it worked, thus sparing themselves from being injured if it did not. At first it occurred to them to effect the result of their principle by pivoting the right and left wings on geared shafts at the stable center of a glider. One wing would turn upward in front when the other turned down, and the balance would readjust. But there seemed to be no way to make this device strong enough without making the glider too heavy. They finally decided on warping or twisting the wings as the simplest and most effective method to effect the result of their principle. (It still would be effective if used today.) The wingtips were to be warped by means of cables controlled by the operator. By warping the wingtips, they expected to vary the inclination of sections of the wings at the tips, and obtain force for restoring balance from the difference in the lifts of the two wingtips.

While twisting a small pasteboard box with opposite ends removed, Wilbur observed that though the vertical sides were rigid endwise, the top and bottom sides could be twisted to have different angles at the opposite ends. Here was a simple means of warping the wings as they intended. They decided that a biplane's wings could be twisted or warped in like manner, enabling them while flying in a glider to warp the wings on the right and left sides to present their surfaces to the air at different angles. By warping the wingtips the operator would be able to increase the angle of attack on one wingtip and decrease it on the other. Thus, they believed, the operator could obtain a greater lift on whichever side he needed it and less lift on the other side in order to assure lateral equilibrium. (They later had to modify this by adding a movable vertical tail.)

To test their principle safely, the brothers built a model glider—actually a kite—with a 5-foot wingspan. Flown as a kite at Dayton, the model glider's wing surfaces were warped by the use of four cords reaching from the upper and lower wingtips on each side to the operator on the ground. Balance from front to rear was maintained in part by an elevator tested variously at the front and rear, as well as by other means. The Wrights believed after the tests that the model glider had demonstrated the efficiency of their system of obtaining both lateral and longitudinal control.

Why Kitty Hawk?

Wilbur and Orville now proposed to build a full-size, man-carrying glider on which to test their method of control. Highly enthusiastic with the idea of gliding as a sport, they started thinking of a place for testing it. To get practice in operating the glider, they would first fly it as a kite before making gliding flights. For kite flying, steady winds and flat, open country were needed; for the gliding, a sandy area for soft landings and sandhill slopes free of

The brothers decided to test their glider at Kitty Hawk after a study of Weather Bureau records and the receipt of this letter.

U. S. Department of Agriculture, Weather Bureau, Office of the Observer. Station: Kitty Hawk NC. Date: Aug 16" 1900.

Mr Wilbur Wright, Dayton Ohio

Dear Sir

In reply to yours of the 3rd I will say the beach here is about one mile wide clear of trees or high hills. Extends for nearly sixty miles same condition. The wind blows mostly from the North & Northeast Sept & October, which is nearly down this piece of land, giving you many miles of a steady wind with a free sweep. I am sorry to say that you could not rent a house here, so you will have to bring tents. You could obtain board. The only way to reach Kitty Hawk is from Manteo Roanoke Island NC in a small sail boat. From your letter I believe you would find it here like you wish. Will be pleased at any time to give you any information. Yours very respectfully, J. J. Dosher

trees and shrubs for low-level flights. The Wrights' hometown of Dayton and its environs were not suitable for extensive glider trials. But because of their business demands, they wanted a site fairly close at hand.

On May 13, 1900, Wilbur wrote his first letter to Chanute asking advice on a suitable location to test a glider. In this letter to the man who became their friend, mentor, and most important correspondent, Wilbur stated:

> For some years I have been afflicted with the belief that flight is possible to man. My disease has increased in severity and I feel that it will soon cost me an increased amount of money if not my life. . . . It is possible to fly without motors, but not without knowledge & skill. This I conceive to be fortunate, for man, by reason of his greater intellect, can more reasonably hope to equal birds in knowledge, than to equal nature in the perfection of her machinery.

Chanute suggested beach locations for glider tests in California, Florida, Georgia, or South Carolina. But after a study of wind records obtained from the Weather Bureau at Washington, the Wrights decided that Kitty Hawk, N.C., seemed to meet their requirements better than any other place within that distance from their home. To confirm this, they wrote to Kitty Hawk, and the replies from Joseph J. Dosher and William J. Tate convinced the brothers that Kitty Hawk was the ideal place for their experiments. They decided to go there as soon as they could build their glider and their bicycle business permitted.

Glider Experiments, 1900

At Dayton, the Wrights began to assemble parts and materials for a full-size, man-carrying glider to test their method of warping the wings to achieve lateral control, and a forward rudder for fore-and-aft balance. In September 1900 Wilbur undertook the journey to Kitty Hawk. Orville followed him later. At the turn of the century such a trip to the isolated village required time and patience. It lies on the Outer Banks of North Carolina between broad Albemarle Sound and the Atlantic Ocean. Then no bridges connected it with the mainland so travel across the sound was by boat.

Wilbur traveled by train from Dayton to Elizabeth City, N.C., the nearest railroad point to his destination. Asking the first persons he chanced to meet about Kitty Hawk he learned that "no one seemed to know anything about the place or how to get there." Those better informed had vexing information: the boat making weekly trips to the Outer Banks had gone the day before. For several days he patiently waited to be dubiously rewarded by passage

Wright camp at Kitty Hawk, 1900. The campsite of 1901-3 was about 4 miles south of this site.

with Israel Perry on a flat-bottom fishing schooner, then anchored 3 miles down the Pasquotank River from the wharf at Elizabeth City.

The small skiff used to take Wilbur from the wharf out to the anchored schooner was loaded almost to the gunwale with three men and supplies. Noticing that the skiff leaked badly, Wilbur asked if it was safe. "Oh," Perry assured him, "it's safer than the big boat." Even so, the schooner managed to sail down the Pasquotank River and through Albemarle Sound safely enough in the rough weather.

It was 9 o'clock the following night before the schooner reached the wharf at Kitty Hawk. Though hungry and aching from the strain of holding on while the schooner rolled and pitched, Wilbur did not go shore until the next morning.

Later, Orville joined Wilbur at Kitty Hawk where both brothers boarded and lodged with the family of William J. Tate until October 4, when they set up their own camp about half a mile away from the village. Native Outer Bankers showed only mild interest

Tom Tate, drumfish, and Wright 1900 glider. A familiar figure in camp, young Tom, on one occasion, was lifted into the air on the glider.

The 1900 glider flying as a kite.

in the Wrights' hopes of flying, but they became excited when they learned that the brothers were keeping in their tent, as fuel for a newfangled gasoline cookstove, the first barrel of gasoline ever taken to the Kitty Hawk area. Fearing an explosion, local folk warily warned their children to keep well away from the brothers' tent. Orville was the cook while in camp; to Wilbur fell the dishwashing chore. Orville always felt that he had the better of the bargain.

The new glider was a double-decker weighing 52 pounds. The 17-foot wingspan gave it a total lifting area of 165 square feet. It cost $15 to make. The uprights were jointed to the top and bottom wings with flexible hinges, and the glider was trussed with steel wires laterally, but not in the fore-and-aft direction. The operator, lying prone on the lower wing to lessen head resistance, maintained lateral equilibrium by tightening a key wire. This in turn tightened every other wire, applying twist to the wingtips—the wing warping principle at full scale. The glider had no tail. Its wing curvature was less than Lilienthal had used.

Wilbur and Orville placed the horizontal operative rudder or elevator in front to provide longitudinal stability. They believed that by placing it in front they would have more up-and-down control to forestall nose dives similar to those that had killed Lilienthal and Pilcher. The Wrights did not invent the elevator. They did use it to more advantage than had earlier experimenters: it was in front of the wings; it was operative instead of fixed; and it flexed to present a convex surface to the air, instead of a flat surface.

The Wrights first flew the glider in the open as a kite. They held it with two ropes and operated the balancing system by cords

The brothers spent 3 days repairing the 1900 glider, wrecked by wind on Oct. 10, 1900.

from the ground. The first day's experiments were attempted with a man on board, using a derrick erected on a hill just south of their camp. The glider was not flown from the derrick again at Kitty Hawk after the first day's tests. On days when the wind was too light to support a man on the glider, they used chain for ballast or flew the machine as a kite in the open without ballast.

Before returning to Dayton, the brothers were determined to try gliding on the side of a hill with a man on board. Four miles south of their camp was a magnificient sand dune about 100 feet high, covering 26 acres, called Kill Devil Hill. They carried their glider to this hill where they made about a dozen free flights down its side.

To take-off from the hillside, one brother and an assistant holding the ends of the glider ran forward against the wind, while the brother who was to operate it ran with them until the machine began to "take hold" of the air, or was airborne. Then the operator jumped aboard and glided free down the hill for 300 or 400 feet, usually gliding only 3 or 4 feet above the soft, sandy ground. The Wrights repeatedly made landings on sledlike skids while moving at a speed of more than 20 miles an hour. The glider was not damaged, nor did the brothers receive any injury. "The machine seemed a rather docile thing," Orville wrote to his sister, from Kitty Hawk, "and we taught it to behave fairly well."

Wilbur and Orville had misread the weather charts they had studied when choosing Kitty Hawk as the location for their experiments. The charts had listed monthly averages, while the day-by-day weather proved to be less than ideal. On some days tests could not be made because of a dead calm; other days the wind blew too strong—up to 45 miles an hour. Orville wrote about the strong winds that blew:

> A little excitement once in a while is not undesirable, but every night, especially when you are so sleepy, it becomes a little monotonous. . . . About two or three nights a week we have to crawl up at ten or eleven o'clock to hold the tent down. . . . We certainly can't complain of the place. We came down here for wind and sand, and we have got them.

Even though the Wrights had only brief spells of favorable weather for practice, they learned much from their experiments. They were pleased with the efficiency of wing-warping to obtain lateral balance, and the horizontal rudder for fore-and-aft control worked better than they had expected. Though Wilbur and Orville believed that fore-and-aft balance and lateral balance were equally important, they were gratified that fore-and-aft balance was so easily attained. They made careful measurements of lift, drag, and angle of attack. The main defect of the glider was its inadequate lifting power. This might be due, the brothers conjectured, to insufficient curvature or camber of the wings which did not have the curvature used by Lilienthal,

Fellow campers at Kill Devil Hills, August 1901. From left: E. C. Huffaker, Octave Chanute, Wilbur Wright, George Spratt.

or perhaps even the Lilienthal tables of air pressure might be in error.

Although important strides had been made toward solving the problem of control, Wilbur and Orville lacked opportunity for sufficient practice since they did not get much time in the air. There still remained much for them to learn before solving the major problems of how to (1) design wings properly, (2) control the aircraft in flight, and (3) provide power, in order to build and fly a powered machine. They knew that they must learn how properly to build and control a glider before attempting to add a motor. "When once a machine is under proper control under all conditions," Wilbur wrote his father from camp, "the motor problem will be quickly solved. A failure of motor will then mean simply a slow descent & safe landing instead of a disastrous fall." They looked forward to the next slack season in the bicycle business so that they might resume experiments with a new glider.

Glider Experiments, 1901

In July 1901 the Wrights returned to Kitty Hawk during a downpour of rain immediately after a storm had broken anemometer cups at 93 miles an hour. There followed a miserable week spent fighting mosquitoes, "which came in a mighty cloud, almost darkening the sun." They attempted to escape by going to bed early, wrapped up in blankets with only noses protruding cautiously from the folds. But the July heat became unbearable beneath the blankets. When they partly uncovered, the mosquitoes again swooped down upon them, forcing a perspiring retreat once more behind blankets. But Wilbur and Orville pushed forward good-humoredly and energetically to solve the problem of flight.

During the 1900–1902 experiments, the Wright family, and the brothers themselves, considered the brother's stay in camp at Kitty Hawk simply as pleasure trips or vacations. Everyone in the family was glad to have them go to their North Carolina camp. The advantages of the sunshine, sea breezes, and outdoor exercise outweighed occasional discomforts and seemed to be good for their health. Indeed, their sister Katharine wrote, "Will and Orv . . . think that life at Kitty Hawk cures all ills, you know."

Being sons of a bishop who enjoined them "to honor the Sabbath," the brothers did not test their gliders on Sundays while in camp. On those days they often visited with the friendly and hospitable people in Kitty Hawk, and at nearby lifesaving stations. They

Wilbur Wright gets an assisted takeoff in the 1901 glider and . . .

. . . sails at low level over one of the Kill Devil Hills.

frequently wrote home. One of Orville's hobbies—photography—also resulted in a fine record of the early experiments. They collected shells and went hunting and fishing. Orville observed while in camp, "This is great country for fishing and hunting. The fish are so thick you see dozens of them whenever you look down into the water."

For living quarters the Wrights continued using a tent. To provide more space they erected a combined glider storage shed and workshop, the building of which they undertook on arrival at camp in 1901. Fresh water was secured nearby by driving a pipe 10 feet or more into the sand.

Their new campsite was located 4 miles south of Kitty Hawk, about 1,000 feet north of Kill Devil Hill, which they had used for gliding the season before and which they now realized offered the best test opportunities. Near the camp were four dunes formed of sand heaped by the winds. These dunes were collectively named Kill Devil Hills. They were constantly changing in height and slope, according to the direction and force of the prevailing winds.

The landing.

The second glider was stored in the wooden shed while the tent served as living quarters at Kill Devil Hills in 1901. Here Wilbur and Orville spent many hours discussing their experiments.

Using three of the four Kill Devil Hills for gliding experiments during the period 1900–1903, the Wrights called these the Big Kill Devil Hill, the West Hill, and the Little Hill.

On the 1901 trip to camp the brothers brought with them parts to be assembled into a larger glider than the one tested in 1900. Knowing it would be impractical to house the larger glider with them in the tent, as they had done with the smaller one, they built a rough frame shed for the new glider and for use as a workshop. This building was 25 feet long and 16 feet wide. Its ends were hinged at the top near the gable parts to form doors so the glider could be removed or stored easily. The doors also served as awnings at the ends of the building.

When assembled, the new glider had a wingspan of 22 feet. It weighed 98 pounds, nearly double the weight of the earlier glider. To give it greater lifting power, the glider had a total lifting area of 290 square feet, considerably larger than the 165-foot wing area of the previous glider. The 1901 glider was a much larger machine than anyone had ever dared try to fly. It had the same system of control and general design as the first one. The Wrights increased the camber in this glider from 1 in 22 to 1 in 12 to conform to the shape prescribed by Lilienthal's tables of air pressure. Chanute and others had used these tables, and the brothers were rudely surprised upon finding that wings with a camber of 1 in 12 were even less efficient than the 1-in-22 camber wings they had used in 1900.

The Wrights were also dismayed to discover that the fore-and aft control was not as effective in a machine with wings of 1-in-12 camber. At times when gliding, they were required to use all their skill and the full power of the rudder to prevent the glider from rearing up so sharply as to lose all headway and then to plunge toward the ground (a dangerous condition which they later referred to as "stalling"—an aeronautical term still in use). The brothers reduced the camber of the wings by adding little "trussing posts" to wires to depress the ribs and flatten the curvature from that used by others to 1 in 18 to make the wings more like those of their 1900 glider. This change resulted in control as good as it had been the year before.

Several hundred glides were made by Wilbur during the 1901 season of experiments. Using the slopes of Kill Devil Hill and West Hill, he sailed along in winds up to 27 miles an hour, breaking all records for distance in gliding. But the brothers were far from satisfied. They had learned a great deal about control, though their glider was still too feeble in lifting itself off the ground and staying aloft.

Occasionally in free flight, the warping of the wings to increase the angle of attack to recover lateral balance did not produce the desired result. The wing having the greater angle sometimes lost speed as it lifted, compared with the opposite wing having a lesser angle. The brothers then realized that the greater angle of the wing on one side gave more resistance to forward motion and reduced the relative speed of that wing. This decrease in speed more than counterbalanced the effect of the larger angle of the wing in producing lift. The Wrights determined that they must add something to their method of controlling equilibrium to insure that equal speeds at the wingtips would be maintained. However, a vertical tail as a solution to the problem was left for the next glider.

Contrary to the scientific texts they had read, it was becoming evident to the Wrights that the travel of the center of pressure on curved or cambered surfaces was not always in the forward direction as on a plane surface. They observed that when the angle of attack on a plane surface was decreased, the center of pressure did move toward the front edge; but on a cambered surface this was true *only when large angles were being decreased.*

Wilbur and Orville were discouraged that the ideas about pressures on curved surfaces and travel of center of pressure, concepts advanced by the most reputable writers on the subject, including Langley, were unreliable. So perplexing did the problem seem that the Wrights considered dropping their experiments altogether. It was apparent, then, that better scientific data were needed before the problems of flight could be solved.

On their way to Dayton from camp, Wilbur declared his belief to Orville that not within a thousand years would man ever fly!

A reproduction of the 1901 wind tunnel that the Wright Brothers used in their shop at Dayton, Ohio. The narrow, metal-bladed fan was belt-operated from the overhead line shafting (top center), forcing a current of air through the tunnel at about 25 miles an hour. This neat workroom is behind the Wright bicycle shop which was moved from Dayton to Greenfield Village, Dearborn, Mich.

He later reduced this prophecy to 50 years. When they made known their discouragement to Chanute he urged the brothers to continue their researches, arguing that if they stopped experimenting it might be a long time before anyone else would come as near to understanding the problem or know how to work toward its solution. The admonitions of Chanute and their own intense interest in scientific inquiry led them to continue their research.

Always practical, the brothers did not take up the problem of flight with the expectation of financial profit, and they had no intention of ruining their bicycle business in pursuit of a dream. When Chanute, who was kept fully informed of their researches, offered financial assistance, Wilbur wrote:

> For the present we would prefer not to accept it for the reason that if we did not feel that the time spent in this work was a dead loss in a financial sense, we would be unable to resist the temptation to devote more time than our business will stand.

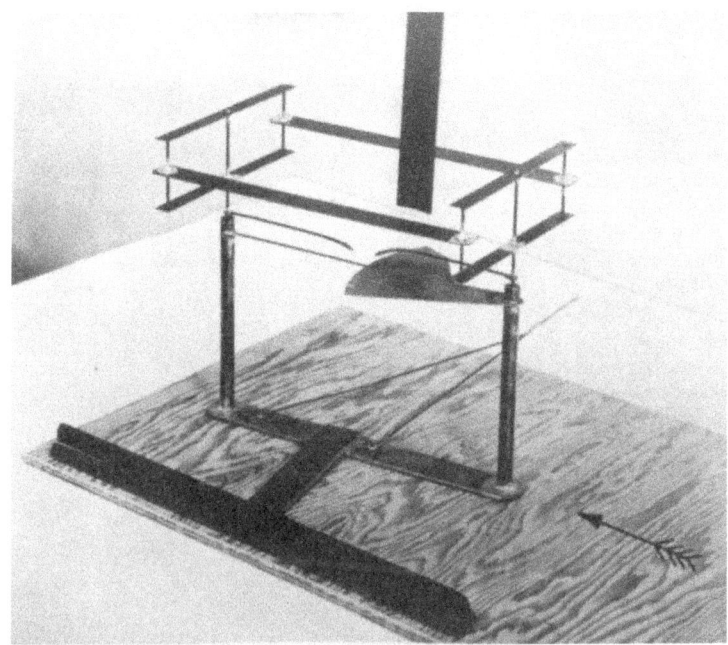

The 1901 drift balance was used for measuring the drag ratio of Wright model airfoils. This is a reproduction. The original balance is in the Franklin Institute, Philadelphia.

Reproduction of lift balance used in 1901 wind tunnel; model airfoil in testing position. The original balance is in the Franklin Institute.

1901 wind-tunnel data sent by Wilbur Wright to Octave Chanute, Jan. 5 and 7, 1902, with instructions for making computations.

Wind-Tunnel Tests, 1901

Shortly after their return to Dayton, the Wrights undertook a series of scientific experiments which produced knowledge that no one had possessed before and that contributed materially to their solution of the problem of powered flight. Disappointed by the relatively poor results achieved at Kitty Hawk with their 1901 glider, in the construction of which they had relied on Lilienthal's and other published tables of air pressures, the Wrights decided to start again from scratch by conducting laboratory tests of their own and by evolving their own air pressure tables from measurements made with model airfoils (miniature wing surfaces) using a simple but effective homemade wind tunnel.

Their second wind tunnel—the first was a makeshift affair hurriedly contrived by Orville out of a wooden starch box and was used for just a few days and then only in preliminary tests—consisted of an open-end wooden box 6 feet long and 16 inches square (inside dimensions). Through this box-like tunnel a flat-bladed fan forced a current of air at a speed of about 25 miles an hour. The air entered the tunnel through a funnel-shaped metal section equipped with a honeycomb-type wind straightener to produce a uniform airflow. The most ingenious parts of the Wright wind tunnel were the two balances they designed for measuring the lift and drag of the model air-foils. Using these balances, the forces could be read as angles from a pointer moving over a protractor fixed to the floor of the tunnel.

In a period of about 2 months toward the close of 1901, the Wrights tested more than 200 surfaces. They measured monoplane, biplane, and triplane wing models. Among these shapes were models of the bird-like wing surfaces used by Lilienthal and the tandem arrangement (in which one wing followed the other) used by Langley. They measured lift and drag forces at various angles from 2° to 45°, tangentials, gliding angles, and lift/drag ratios; they tested the effect of aspect ratio and the effect on lift of varying the camber of curvature of the surfaces, and tried a variety of shapes and thicknesses for the leading and trailing edges, for wing-tips, and for such structural members as uprights.

As a result of these experiments, all carefully carried out and minutely recorded, they obtained a body of data on air pressures and on the aerodynamic properties of wings, control surfaces, and structural parts. The extent and reliability of the information from these tests far exceeded anything that had ever been available to other experimenters or was to be available for at least another decade. Their friend and correspondent, Octave Chanute, marveled at the speed and accuracy with which this laboratory research was carried out.

Wilbur Wright in Kill Devil Hills camp building before it was remodeled by adding space for living quarters, Aug. 29, 1902. (1901 glider at right.)

The Wrights themselves soon came to realize that these scientific experiments, on which they had embarked with considerable reluctance, were in fact the most valuable part of all their work in that they gave them accounts and detailed knowledge on which to base the design of flying machines.

The wind-tunnel experiments concluded in December 1901 made it possible for the Wrights to abandon the trial-and-error method of construction that had gone into their 1900 and 1901 gliders and to solve the basic problem of the correct design for lifting wings. Now they were able to devote their time to the two other major problems that had to be solved before human flight could be accomplished: a system for obtaining full control in the air, and the addition of an engine and propellers to the aircraft.

Glider Experiments, 1902

The Wrights had faith in the tables of air pressure compiled from their wind-tunnel experiments. Their new knowledge was incorporated into a larger glider which they built based on the aerodynamic data they had gained. Now they wanted to verify those findings by actual gliding experiments. At the end of August 1902, they were back in camp at Kill Devil Hills for the third season of experiments. Battered by winter gales, their camp needed repairing. They decided to build a 15-foot addition to the combined workshop and glider-storage shed to use as a kitchen and living quarters. Their new living quarters were "royal luxuries" when compared with the tent facilities of previous camps.

The new glider had a wingspan of 32 feet, 1 inch; a considerable increase over the wingspan of 22 feet for the 1901 glider. Its lifting area, 305 square feet, was not much greater than the glider of the previous year. Their wind-tunnel experiments having demonstrated the importance of aspect ratio, the brothers made the wingspan about six times the chord or fore-and-aft measurement instead of three. Weighing 112 pounds, the glider was 16 feet, 1 inch long. In the 1900 and 1901 gliders, the wing-warping mechanism had been worked by movement of the operator's feet. In the 1902 glider this mechanism operated by sidewise movement of the operator's hips resting in a cradle on the lower wing. Wilbur wrote his father from camp, "Our new machine is a very great improvement over anything we had built before and over anything any one has built."

Kitchen in the living quarters of the remodeled camp building at Kill Devil Hills, 1902

One of the successful glides made in October 1903 with the 1902 glider, camp buildings in distance.

This was the first Wright glider to have a tail, consisting of fixed twin vertical vanes, as well as a front rudder. The tail's purpose was to overcome the turning difficulties encountered in some of the flights with the 1901 glider by maintaining equal speeds at the two wingtips when the wings were warped. The tail was expected to counterbalance the difference in resistance of the two wingtips. If the wing on one side tended to swerve forward, then the Wrights thought the tail, being more exposed to the wind on the same side, should stop the glider from turning farther.

The tail on this glider, however, caused a new problem that had not occurred in their previous gliders. At times, when struck by a side gust of wind, the glider turned up sidewise and came sliding laterally to the ground in spite of the effort and skill of the operator in using the warping mechanism to control it. The brothers were experiencing tailspins, though that term did not come into use until several years later. When tailspins occurred, the glider would sometimes slide so fast that the movement caused the tail's fixed vertical vanes to aggravate the turning movement instead of counteracting it by maintaining an equal speed at the opposite wingtips.

Wilbur Wright making right turn in glide from West Hill, Oct. 24, 1902.
(Kill Devil Hill in background.)

High glide on Oct. 10, 1902.   *Courtesy, Smithsonian Institution.*

The result was worse than if there were no fixed vertical tail.

While lying awake one night, Orville thought of converting their vertical tail from two fixed vanes to a single movable rudder. When making a turn or recovering lateral balance, this rudder could be moved toward the low wing to compensate for the increased drag imparted to the high wing by its greater angle of attack. Wilbur listened attentively when Orville told him about the idea the next morning. Then, without hesitation, Wilbur not only agreed to the change but immediately proposed the further important modification of interconnecting the rudder control wires with those of the wing-warping. Thus by a single movement the operator could effect both controls. Through the brilliant interplay of two inventive minds, all the essentials of the Wright control system were completed within a few hours.

The combination of warp and rudder control became the key to successful control of their powered machine and to the control of all aircraft since. (Modern airplanes—and indeed Wright planes after the middle of their 1905 experimental season—do not have the aileron and rudder controls permanently interconnected, but these controls can be and are operated in combination when necessary.) Together with the use of the forward elevator, it allowed the Wrights to perform all the basic aerial maneuvers that were necessary for controlled flight. The essential problem of how to control a flying machine about all three axes was now solved.

The trials of the 1902 glider were successful beyond expectation. Nearly 1,000 glider flights were made by the Wrights from Kill Devil, West, and Little Hills. A number of their glides were of more than 600 feet, and a few of them were against a 36-mile-an-hour wind. Flying in winds so strong required great skill on the part of the operator. No previous experimenter had ever dared to try gliding in so stiff a wind. Orville wrote his sister, "We now hold all the records! The largest machine we handled in any kind [of weather, made the longest dis]tance glide (American), the longest time in the air, the smallest angle of descent, and the highest wind!!!" Their record glide for distance was 622½ feet in 26 seconds. Their record glide for angle was an angle of 5° for a glide of 156 feet. The 1902 glider had about twice the dynamic efficiency of any other glider ever built up to that time anywhere in the world.

By the end of the 1902 season of experiments, the Wrights had solved two of the major problems: how properly to design wings and control surfaces and how to control a flying machine about its three axes. Most of the battle was now won. There remained only the major problem of adding the engine and propellers. Before leaving camp, the brothers began designing a new and still larger machine to be powered with a motor.

It was the 1902 glider that the Wrights pictured and described in the drawings and specifications of their patent, which they applied for in March of the following year. Their patent was established, through the action of the courts in the United States and abroad, as the basic or pioneer airplane patent.

The Motor and the Propellers

Home again in Dayton, the Wrights were ready to carry out plans begun in camp at Kill Devil Hills for a powered machine. They invited bids for a gasoline engine which would develop 8 to 9 horsepower, weigh no more than 180 pounds or an average of 20 pounds per horsepower, and be free of vibrations. None of the manufacturers to whom they wrote was able to supply them with a motor light enough to meet these specifications. The Wrights therefore designed and built their own motor, with their mechanic, Charles E. Taylor, giving them enthusiastic help in the construction.

The engine body and frame of the first "little gas motor" which they began building in December 1902 broke while being tested. Rebuilding the light-weight motor, they shop-tested it in May 1903.

The Wright motor used in the first flights of Dec. 17, 1903, after its reconstruction in 1928.

In its final form the motor used in the first powered flights had 4 horizontal cylinders of 4-inch bore and 4-inch stroke, with an aluminum-alloy crankcase and water jacket. The fuel tank had a capacity of four-tenths of a gallon of gasoline. The entire power plant including the engine, magneto, radiator, tank, water, fuel, tubing, and accessories weighed a little more than 200 pounds.

Owing to certain peculiarities of design, after several minutes' run the engine speed dropped to less than 75 percent of what it was on cranking the motor. The highest engine speed measured developed 15.76 horsepower at 1,200 revolutions per minute in the first 15 seconds after starting the cold motor. After several minutes' run

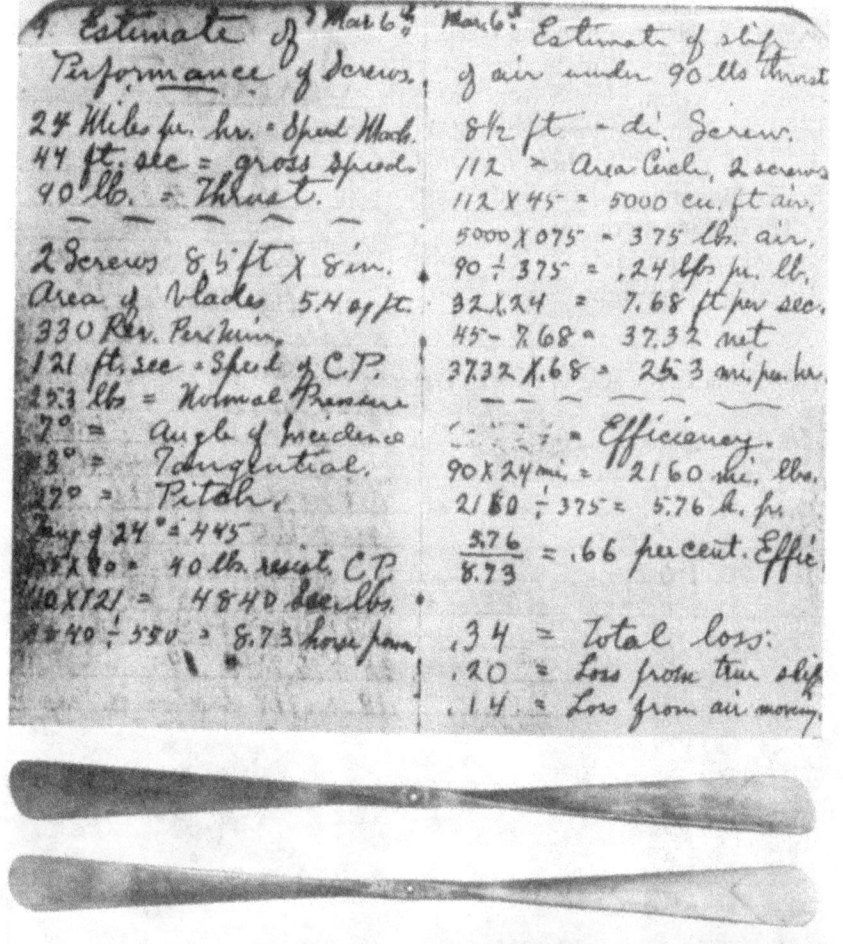

Propeller estimates, made by the Wrights 8 months before the flights of December 1903. Their formulas resulted in the highly efficient propellers which were used in the first Wright Flyer. These were 8½ feet from one canvas-covered tip to the other. Top view shows the front, bottom view, the rear.

the number of revolutions dropped rapidly to 1,090 per minute, developing 11.81 brake horsepower. Even so, the Wrights were pleasantly surprised since they had not counted on more than 8 horsepower capable of driving a machine weighing only about 625 pounds. Having a motor with a power output of about 12 horsepower instead of 8, the Wrights could build the machine to have a larger total weight than 625 pounds.

The motor was started with the aid of a dry-battery coil box. After starting, ignition was provided by a low-tension magneto, friction-driven by the flywheel. No pump was used in the cooling system. The vertical sheet-steel radiator was attached to the central forward upright of the machine.

When the brothers began to consider designing propellers, they unhappily discovered that the forces in action on aerial propellers had never been correctly resolved or defined. Since they did not have sufficient time or funds to develop an efficient propeller by the more costly trial-and-error means, it was necessary for them to study the screw propeller from a theoretical standpoint. By studying the problem, they hoped to develop a theory from which to design the propellers for the powered machine. The problem was not easy, as the Wrights wrote:

> What at first seemed a simple problem became more complex the longer we studied it. With the machine moving forward, the air flying backward, the propellers turning sidewise, and nothing standing still, it seemed impossible to find a starting point from which to trace the various simultaneous reactions. Contemplation of it was confusing. After long arguments we often found ourselves in the ludicrous position of each having been converted to the other's side, with no more agreement than when the discussion began.

However, in a few months the brothers untangled the conflicting factors and calculations. After studying the problem, they felt sure of their ability to design propellers of exactly the right diameter, pitch, and area for their need. Estimates derived from their formulas led to their propellers operating at a higher rate of efficiency (66 percent) than any others of that day. The tremendous expenditure of power that characterized experiments of other aeronautical investigators up to that time were due to inefficient propellers as well as inefficient lifting surfaces.

The Wright propellers, designed according to their own calculations, were the first propellers ever built by anyone for which the performance could be predicted. After tests, their propellers produced not quite 1 percent less thrust than they had calculated. In useful work they gave about two thirds of the power expended—a third more than had been achieved by such men as Sir Hiram Maxim and Dr. Langley.

Arrangement of propeller-driving chains and casings on original Wright 1903 machine displayed in the Smithsonian Institution. *Courtesy, Smithsonian Institution.*

The brothers decided to use two propellers on their powered machine for two reasons. First, by using two propellers they could secure a reaction against a greater quantity of air and use a larger pitch angle than was possible with one propeller; and second, having the two propellers run in opposite directions, the gyroscopic action of one would neutralize that of the other. The two pusher-type propellers on the 1903 powered machine were mounted on tubular shafts about 10 feet apart, both driven by chains running over sprockets. By crossing one of the chains in a figure eight, the propellers were run in opposite directions to counteract torque. The propellers were made of three laminations of spruce, each 1⅛ inches thick. The wood was glued together and shaped with a hatchet and drawshave.

The Powered Machine, 1903

The 1903 machine had a wingspan of 40 feet, 4 inches; a camber of 1 in 20; a wing area of 510 square feet; and a length of 21 feet, 1 inch. It weighed 605 pounds without a pilot. The machine was not symmetrical from side to side; the engine was placed on the lower wing to the right of center to reduce the danger of its falling on the pilot. The pilot would ride lying prone as on the gliders, but to the left of center to balance the weight. The right wing was approximately 4 inches longer than the left to provide additional lift to compensate for the engine which weighed 34 pounds more than the pilot.

Fore-and-aft control was by means of the elevator in front, operated by hand lever. The tail of the machine had twin movable rudders instead of a single movable rudder developed in the 1902 glider. These rudders were linked by wires to the wing-warping system. Their coordinated control mechanism was worked by wires attached to a cradle on the lower wing, in which the pilot lay prone. To turn the machine to the left, the pilot moved his body, and with it the cradle, a few inches to the left. This caused the rear right wingtips to be pulled down or warped (thus giving more lift and raising them) and the rear left wingtips to move upward, and at the same time the coordinating mechanism introduced enough left rudder to compensate for yaw. The rudder counteracted the added resistance of the wing with the greater angle and the resulting tendency of the machine to swing in the opposite direction to the desired left turn, as well as aiding the turn on its own account.

On September 25, 1903, the Wrights arrived once more at their Kill Devil Hills camp. They repaired and again used the living quarters which they had added to the storage building in 1902, called their "summer house." Their 1902 glider, which they had left

Wright 1903 machine (rear view) in the Smithsonian Institution showing attachments on the lower wing. *Courtesy, Smithsonian Institution.*

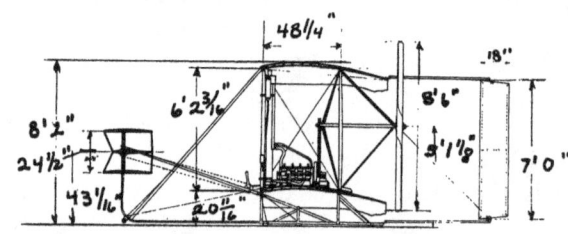

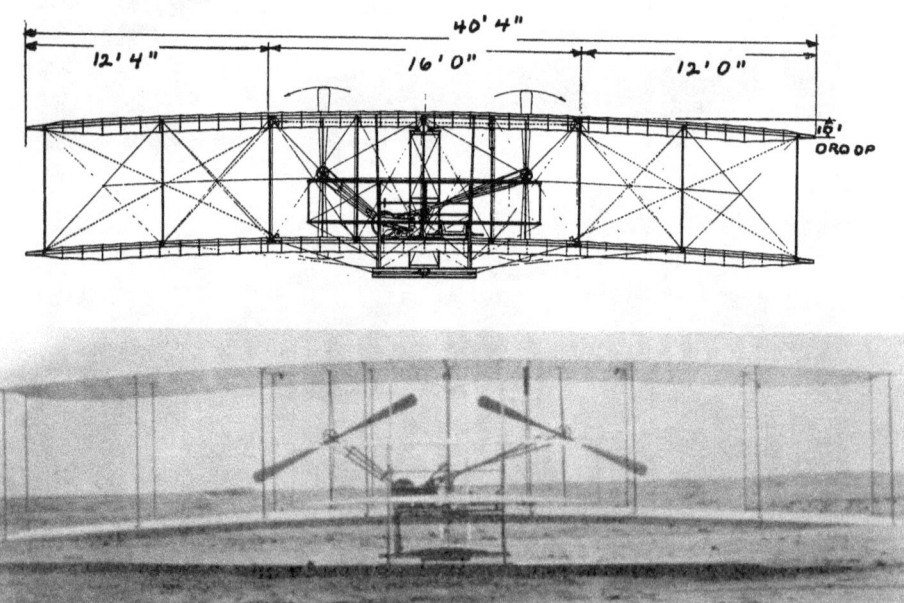

stored in this building after that season of experiments, was again housed with them in the building. They erected a new building to house the powered machine alongside the glider-storage and living-quarters building and commenced the chore of assembling the powered machine in its new hangar. Occasionally they took the 1902 glider out for practice. After a few trials each brother was able to make a new world's record by gliding for more than a minute.

The first weeks in camp were a time of vicissitudes for the Wrights. Assembling the machine and installing the engine and propellers proved an arduous task. When tested, the motor missed so often that the vibrations twisted one of the propeller shafts and jerked the assembly apart. Both shafts had to be sent back to their Dayton bicycle shop to be made stronger. After they had been returned, one broke again, and Orville had to carry the shafts back to Dayton to make new ones of more durable material. The magneto failed to produce a strong enough spark. A stubborn problem was fastening the sprockets to the propeller shafts; the sprockets and the nuts loosened within a few seconds even when they were tightened with a 6-foot lever.

It was then that the weather acted as if it were threatening the brothers not to venture into a new element. A gale swept over their

Opposite page and below: Plans of the Wright Brothers 1903 plane and photographs of front and side views of the plane. *Plans, courtesy, Smithsonian Institution.*

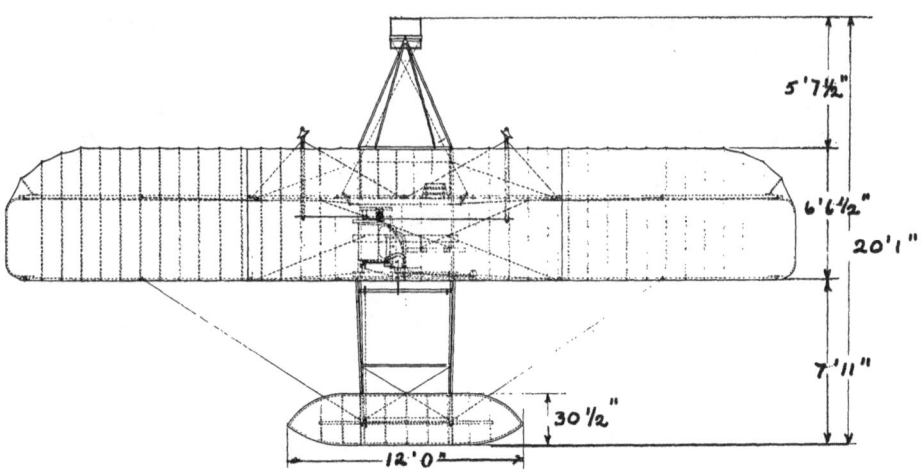

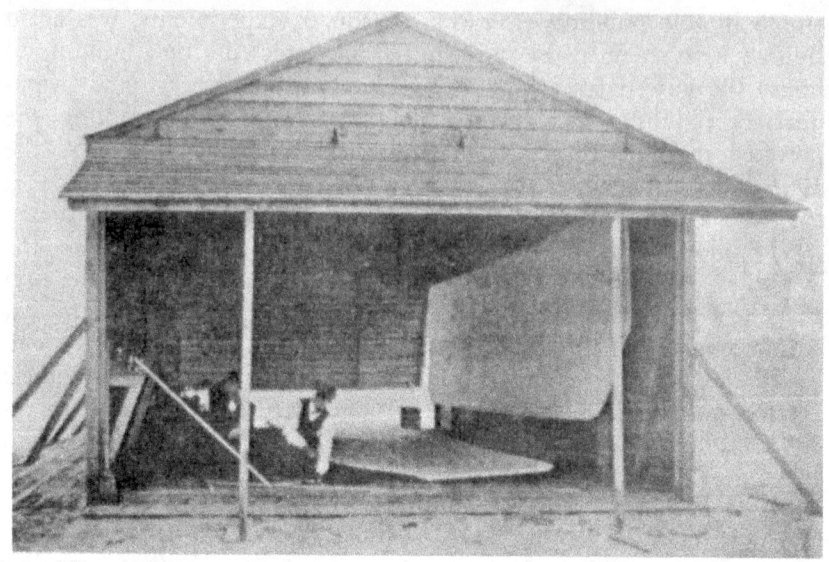

Assembling the 1903 machine in the new camp building at Kill Devil Hills, October 1903.

camp with winds up to 75 miles an hour. As their living quarters rocked with the wind, and rainwater flowed over part of the floor, the Wrights expected to hear the new hangar building next door, which housed the powered machine, crash over completely. "The wind and rain continued through the night," related Wilbur to his sister, "but we took the advice of the Oberlin coach, 'Cheer up, boys, there is no hope,' We went to bed, and both slept soundly."

It became so cold that the brothers had to make a heater from a drum used to hold carbide. Wilbur assured his father:

> However we are entirely comfortable, and have no trouble keeping warm at nights. In addition to the classifications of last year, to wit, 1, 2, 3, and 4 blanket nights, we now have 5 blanket nights, & 5 blankets & 2 quilts. Next come 5 blankets, 2 quilts & fire; then 5, 2, fire, & hot-water jug. This as far as we have got so far.

The 1903 machine and camp buildings at Kill Devil Hills, Nov. 24, 1903.

At last the weather cleared, the engine began to purr, their handmade heater functioned better after improvements, and, with the help of a tire cement they had used in their bicycle shop, they "stuck those sprockets so tight I doubt whether they will ever come loose again." Chanute visited their camp for a few days and wrote November 23, "I believe the new machine of the Wrights to be the most promising attempt at flight that has yet been made." Both brothers sensed that the goal was in sight.

The powered machine's undercarriage (landing gear) consisted of two runners, or sledlike skids, instead of wheels. These were extended farther out in front of the wings than were the landing skids on the gliders to guard against the machine rolling over in landing. Four feet, eight inches apart, the two runners were ideal for landing as skids on the soft beach sands. But for take-offs, it was necessary to build a single-rail starting track 60 feet long on which ran a small truck which held the machine about 8 inches off the ground. The easily movable starting rail was constructed of four 15-foot 2 x 4's set on edge, with the upper surface topped by a thin strip of metal.

The truck which supported the skids of the plane during the takeoff consisted of two parts: a crossbeam plank about 6 feet long laid across a smaller piece of wood forming the truck's undercarriage which moved along the track on two rollers made from modified bicycle hubs. For take-offs, the machine was lifted onto the truck with the plane's undercarriage skids resting on the two opposite ends of the crossbeam. A modified bicycle hub was attached to the forward crosspiece of the plane between its skids to prevent the machine from nosing over on the launching track. A wire from the truck attached to the end of the starting track held the plane back while the engine was warmed up. Then the restraining wire was released by the pilot. The airplane, riding on the truck, started forward along the rail. If all went well, the machine was airborne and hence lifted off the truck before reaching the end of the starting track; while the truck, remaining on the track, continued on and ran off the rail.

With the new propeller shafts installed, the powered machine was ready for its first testing on December 12. However, the wind was too light for the machine to take-off from the level ground near their camp with a run of only 60 feet permitted by the starting track. Nor did they have enough time before dark to take the machine to one of the nearby Kill Devil Hills, where, by placing the track on a steeply inclined slope, enough speed could be promptly attained for starting in calm air. The following day was Sunday, which the brothers spent resting and reading, hoping for suitable weather for flying the next day so that they could be home by Christmas.

On December 14 it was again too calm to permit a start from level ground near the camp. The Wrights, therefore, decided to take

The first Wright Flyer rests on the starting track at Kill Devil Hill prior to the trial of Dec. 14, 1903. The four men from the Kill Devil Hills Life Saving Station helped move the machine from the campsite to the hill. The two boys ran home on hearing the engine start.

the machine to the north side of Kill Devil Hill about a quarter of a mile away to make their first attempt to fly in a power-driven machine. They had arranged to signal nearby life-savers to inform them when the first trial was ready to start. A signal was placed on one of the camp buildings that could be seen by personnel on duty about a mile away at the Kill Devil Hills Life Saving Station.

The Wrights were soon joined by five lifesavers who helped to transport the machine from camp to Kill Devil Hill. Setting the 605-pound machine on the truck atop the starting track, they ran the truck to the end of the track and added the rear section of the track to the front end. By relaying sections of the track, the machine rode on the truck to the site chosen for the test, 150 feet up the side of the hill.

The truck, with the machine thereon, facing downhill, was fastened with a wire to the end of the starting track, so that it could not start until released by the pilot. The engine was started to make sure it was in proper condition. Two small boys, with a dog, who had come with the lifesavers, "made a hurried departure over the hill for home on hearing the engine start." Each brother was eager for the chance to make the first trial, so a coin was tossed to determine which of them it should be; Wilbur won.

Wilbur took his place as pilot while Orville held a wing to steady the machine during the run on the track. The restraining wire was released, the machine started forward quickly on the rail, leaving Orville behind. After a run of 35 or 40 feet, the airplane took off. Wilbur turned the machine up too suddenly after leaving the track, before it had gained enough speed. It climbed a few feet, stalled, and settled to the ground at the foot of the hill after being in the air just 3½ seconds. This trial was considered unsuccessful

Wilbur Wright in damaged machine near the base of Kill Devil Hill after unsuccessful trial of Dec. 14, 1903. Repairs were completed by the afternoon of December 16, but poor wind conditions prevented another trial until the following day.

Crew members of the Kill Devil Hills Life Saving Station, about 1900. In 1903, lifesavers from this station witnessed the attempt on December 14 and saw the successful flights of December 17.

because the machine landed at a point at the base of the hill many feet lower than that from which it had started on the side of the hill. Wilbur wrote of his trial:

> However the real trouble was an error in judgment, in turning up too suddenly after leaving the track, and as the machine had barely speed enough for support already, this slowed it down so much that before I could correct the error, the machine began to come down, though turned up at a big angle. Toward the end it began to speed up again but it was too late, and it struck the ground while moving a little to one side, due to wind and a rather bad start.

In landing, one of the skids and several other parts were broken, preventing a second attempt that day. Repairs were completed by noon of the 16th, but the wind was too calm to fly the machine that afternoon. The brothers, however, were confident of soon making a successful flight. "There is now no question of final success," Wilbur wrote his father, though Langley had recently made two attempts to fly and had failed in both. "This did not disturb or hurry us in the least," Orville commented on Langley's attempts. "We knew that he had to have better scientific data than was contained in his published works to successfully build a man-carrying flying machine."

December 17, 1903: The Day Man First Flew

Thursday, December 17 dawned, and was to go down in history as a day when a great engineering feat was accomplished. It was a cold day with winds of 22 to 27 miles an hour blowing from the north. Puddles of water near the camp were covered with ice. The Wrights waited indoors, hoping the winds would diminish. But they continued brisk, and at 10 in the morning the brothers decided to attempt a flight, fully realizing the difficulties and dangers of flying a relatively untried machine in so high a wind.

In strong winds, hills were not needed to launch the machine, since the force of the winds would enable the machine to take off on the short starting track from level ground. Indeed, the winds were almost too gusty to launch the machine at all that day, but the brothers estimated that the added dangers while in flight would be compensated in part by the slower speed in landing caused by flying into stiff winds. As a safety precaution, they decided to fly as close to the ground as possible. They were superb flyers, courageous, but never foolhardy.

A signal was again displayed to notify the men at the Kill Devil Hills Life Saving Station that further trials were intended. They took the machine out of the hanger, and laid the 60-foot starting

Getting ready for the first flight, Dec. 17, 1903. From a diorama in the Wright Brothers National Memorial Visitor Center.

track in a south-to-north direction on a smooth stretch of level ground less than 100 feet west of the hanger and more than 1,000 feet north of Kill Devil Hill. They chose this location for the trials because the ground had recently been covered with water, and because it was so level that little preparation was necessary to lay the track. Both the starting track and the machine resting on the truck faced directly into the north wind. The restraining wire was attached from the truck to the south end of the track.

Before the brothers were quite ready to fly the machine, John T. Daniels, Willie S. Dough, and Adam D. Etheridge, personnel from the Kill Devil Hills Life Saving Station, arrived to see the trials; with them came William C. Brinkley of Manteo, and John T. Moore, a boy from Nags Head. The right to the first trial belonged to Orville; Wilbur had used his turn in the unsuccessful attempt on December 14. Orville put his camera on a tripod before climbing aboard the machine, and told Daniels to press the button when the machine had risen directly in front of the camera.

After running the engine and propellers a few minutes, the take-off attempt was ready. At 10:35 a.m., Orville lay prone on the lower wing with hips in the cradle that operated the control mechanisms. He released the restraining wire and the machine started down the 60-foot track, traveling slowly into the headwind at about 7 or 8 miles an hour—so slow that Wilbur was able to run along-side holding the right wing to balance the machine on the track. After a run of 40 feet on the track, the machine took off. When the airplane had risen about 2 feet above ground, Daniels snapped the famous photograph of the conquest of the air. The plane then climbed 10 feet into the sky, while Orville struggled with the controlling mechanisms to keep it from rising too high in such an irregular, gusty wind.

The first flight.

Orville sought to fly a level flight course, though buffeted by the strong headwind. However, when turning the rudder up or down, the plane turned too far either way and flew an erratic up-and-down course, first quickly rising about 10 feet, then suddenly darting close to the ground. The first successful flight ended with a sudden dart to the ground after having flown 120 feet from the take-off point in 12 seconds time at a groundspeed of 6.8 miles an hour and an airspeed of 30 miles an hour. In the words of Orville Wright:

> This flight lasted only 12 seconds, but it was nevertheless the first in the history of the world in which a machine carrying a man had raised itself by its own power into the air in full flight, had sailed forward without reduction of speed, and had finally landed at a point as high as that from which it started.

Orville found that the new, almost untried, controlling mechanisms operated more powerfully than the previous controls he had used in gliders. He also learned that the front rudder was balanced too near the center. Because of its tendency to turn itself when started, the unfamiliar powered machine's front rudder turned more than was necessary.

The airplane had been slightly damaged on landing. Quick repairs were made. With the help of the onlookers, the machine was brought back to the track and prepared for a second flight. Wilbur took his turn at 11:20 a.m., and flew about 175 feet in about 12 seconds. He also flew an up-and-down course, similar to the first flight, while operating the unfamiliar controls. The speed over the ground during the second flight was slightly faster than that of the first flight because

Third flight of Dec. 17, 1903, Orville Wright at the controls. No photograph was taken of the day's second flight, in which Wilbur Wright was operator.

End of fourth and longest flight of Dec. 17, 1903. Distance: 852 feet; time: 59 seconds.

Close-up of 1903 machine at end of last flight, rudder frame broken in landing.
Courtesy, Smithsonian Institution.

Orville Wright's diary showing Dec. 17, 1903 entry. This account is the only contemporary written record of these momentous flights.

the winds were diminishing. The airplane was carried back to the starting track and prepared for a third flight.

At 11:40 a.m., Orville made the third flight, flying a steadier course than that of the two previous flights. All was going nicely when a sudden gust of wind from the side lifted the airplane higher by 12 to 15 feet, turning it sidewise in an alarming manner. With the plane flying sidewise, Orville warped the wingtips to recover lateral balance, and pointed the plane down to land as quickly as possible. The new lateral control was more effective than he had

(Orville Wright's diary—December 17 entry, continued)

expected. The plane not only leveled off, but the wing that had been high dropped more than he had intended, and it struck the ground shortly before the plane landed. The third flight was about 200 feet in about 15 seconds.

Wilbur started on the fourth flight at noon. He flew the first few hundred feet on an up-and-down course similar to the first two flights. But after flying 300 feet from the take-off point, the airplane was brought under control. The plane flew a fairly even course for an additional 500 feet, with little undulation to disturb its level flight. While in flight about 800 feet from the take-off point, the airplane commenced pitching again, and, in one of its

(Orville Wright's diary—December 17 entry, continued)

darts downward, struck the ground. The fourth flight measured 852 feet over the ground; the time in the air was 59 seconds.

The four successful flights made on December 17 were short because the Wrights, not desiring to fly a new machine at much height in strong winds, sometimes found it impossible to correct the up-and-down motion of the airplane before it struck the ground. Wilbur remarked:

> Those who understand the real significance of the conditions under which we worked will be surprised rather at the length than the shortness of the flights made with an unfamiliar machine after less than one

(Orville Wright's diary—December 17 entry, continued)

minute's practice. The machine possesses greater capacity of being controlled than any of our former machines.

They carried the airplane back to camp and set it up a few feet west of the hangar. While the Wrights and onlookers were discussing the flights, a sudden gust of wind struck the plane and turned it over a number of times, damaging it badly. The airplane could not be repaired in time for any more flights that year; indeed, it was never flown again. Daniels gained the dubious honor of becoming the first airplane casualty when he was slightly scratched and bruised while caught inside the machine between the wings in an attempt to stop the plane as it rolled over. Subsequent events were vivid in Daniels' mind while reminiscing of his "first—and God help me—my last flight." He relates:

> I found myself caught in them wires and the machine blowing across the beach heading for the ocean, landing first on one end and then on the other, rolling over and over, and me getting more tangled up in it all the time. I tell you, I was plumb scared. When the thing did stop for half a second I nearly broke up every wire and upright getting out of it.

Orville made this matter-of-fact entry in his diary: "After dinner we went to Kitty Hawk to send off telegram to M. W. While there we called on Capt. and Mrs. Hobbs, Dr. Cogswell and the station men." Toward evening that day Bishop Milton Wright in Dayton received the telegram from his sons:

> Success four flights Thursday morning all against twenty-one mile wind started from level with engine power alone average speed through air thirty-one miles longest 57 seconds inform press home Christmas. Orevelle Wright.

In the transmission of the telegram, 57 seconds was incorrectly given for the 59-second record flight, and Orville's name was misspelled. The Norfolk telegraph operator leaked the news to a local paper, the *Virginian-Pilot*. The resulting story produced a series of false reports as to the length and duration of the December 17 flights. Practically none of the information contained in the telegram was used, except that the Wrights had flown.

The Bishop gave out a biographical note:

> Wilbur is 36, Orville 32, and they are as inseparable as twins. For several years they have read up on aeronautics as a physician would read his books, and they have studied, discussed, and experimented together. Natural workmen, they have invented, constructed, and operated their gliders, and finally their 'Wright Flyer,' jointly, all at their own personal expense. About equal credit is due each.

The world took little note of the Wrights' tremendous achievement and years passed before its full significance was realized. After reading the Wrights' telegram, the Associated Press representative in Dayton remarked, "Fifty-seven seconds, hey? If it had been fifty-seven minutes then it might have been a news item." Three years after the first flight an editorial appeared in the December 15, 1906, issue of the *Scientific American,* which included the following:

> In all the history of invention, there is probably no parallel to the unostentatious manner in which the Wright brothers of Dayton, Ohio, ushered into the world their epoch-making invention of the first successful aeroplane flying-machine.

form No. 168.
THE WESTERN UNION TELEGRAPH COMPANY.
──── INCORPORATED ────
23,000 OFFICES IN AMERICA.   CABLE SERVICE TO ALL THE WORLD.

This Company TRANSMITS and DELIVERS messages only on conditions limiting its liability, which have been assented to by the sender of the following message.
Errors can be guarded against only by repeating a message back to the sending station for comparison, and the Company will not hold itself liable for errors or delays
in transmission or delivery of Unrepeated Messages, beyond the amount of tolls paid thereon, nor in any case where the claim is not presented in writing within sixty days
after the message is filed with the Company for transmission.
This is an UNREPEATED MESSAGE, and is delivered by request of the sender, under the conditions named above.
ROBERT C. CLOWRY, President and General Manager.

RECEIVED at   170

176 C KA CS 33 Paid.   Via Norfolk   Va

Kitty Hawk N C Dec 17

Bishop M Wright

7 Hawthorne St

Success four flights thursday morning   all against twenty one mile

wind started from Level with engine power alone average speed

through air thirty one miles longest 57 seconds inform Press

home ##### Christmas .   Orevelle Wright   525P

Orville Wright wired his father to announce the successful flights of Dec. 17, 1903.

After the First Flight

After 1903, the Wrights carved brilliant careers in aeronautics and helped found the aviation industry. The successful flights made at Kill Devil Hills in December 1903 encouraged them to make improvements on a new plane called Flyer No. 2. About 100 flights were flown near Dayton in 1904. These totaled only 45 minutes in the air, although they made two 5-minute flights. Experimenting chiefly with control and maneuver, many complete circuits of the small flying field were made.

A new and improved plane, Flyer No. 3, was built in 1905. On October 5 they made a record flight of 24⅕ miles, while the plane was in the air 38 minutes and 3 seconds. The era of the airplane was well on the way. The lessons and successes at Kill Devil Hills in December 1903 were fast making the crowded skies of the Air Age possible.

Believing their invention was now perfected for practical use, the Wrights wanted the United States Government to have a world monopoly on their patents, and more important, on all the aerodynamic, design, and pilotage secrets they knew relating to the airplane. As early as 1905 they had received overtures from representatives of foreign governments. The United States Army turned down their

Orville Wright in 1904 flight 85 at Huffman Prairie near Dayton, November 16. Distance: approximately 1,760 feet; time: 45 seconds.

1905 flight 41—Orville's 12-mile flight of September 29.

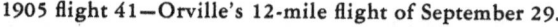

1905 flight 46, October 4—20.8 miles in 33.3 minutes, the second longest flight of 1905. It was exceeded only by the 24-mile flight of October 5. The era of the airplane was well on its way.

Orville Wright (1871–1948) taken about 1908.

first offers without making an effort to investigate whether the airplane had been brought to a stage of practical operation. But disbelief was on the wane. In February 1908 the United States War Department made a contract with the brothers for an airplane. Only 3 weeks later the Wrights closed a contract with a Frenchman to form a syndicate for the rights to manufacture, sell, or license the use of the Wright airplane in France.

During their Dayton experiments, the Wrights had continued to pilot their airplanes while lying prone with hips in the cradle on the lower wing. Now they adopted a different arrangement of the control levers to be used in a sitting position and added a seat for a passenger. The brothers brought their airplane to Kill Devil Hills in April 1908 to practice handling the new arrangement of the control levers. They wanted to be prepared for the public trials to be made for the United States Government, near Washington, and for the company in France.

They erected a new building at Kill Devil Hills to house the airplane and to live in, because storms the year before had nearly demolished their 1903 camp buildings. Between May 6 and May 14, 1908, the Wrights made 22 flights at their old testing grounds. On May 14 the first flight with two men aboard a plane was made near West Hill; Wilbur Wright being the pilot, and Charles Furnas, a mechanic, the passenger. Orville and Furnas then made a flight

Wilbur Wright (1867–1912) taken about 1908.

together of over 2 miles, passing between Kill Devil Hill and West Hill, and turning north near the sound to circle Little Hill before returning over the starting point close to their camp to land near West Hill on the second lap.

Byron R. Newton, a newspaper reporter, was concealed in the woods with other newsmen near camp to watch the Wrights fly. Newton predicted in his diary just after seeing his first flight: "Some day Congress will erect a monument here to these Wrights." Nineteen years later the Congress established the area as a National Memorial.

Wilbur journeyed to France after completing the tests at Kill Devil Hills, while Orville returned home to complete the construction of an airplane for the United States Government. As Wilbur set about methodically to assemble his airplane at Le Mans, some 125 miles from Paris, skeptics greeted the delay by accusing him of bluffing. But Wilbur refused to hurry. *"Le bluff continue,"* cried a Paris newspaper. However, when Wilbur took off on August 8, circling the field to come in for a perfect landing, the crowd could scarcely believe its eyes. Skeptics were confounded, and enthusiasm was uproarious.

Wilbur's complete lack of conceit, together with his decency and intelligence, won from the French people a hero-worship attitude, while the press was unsparing in its praise and lamented having

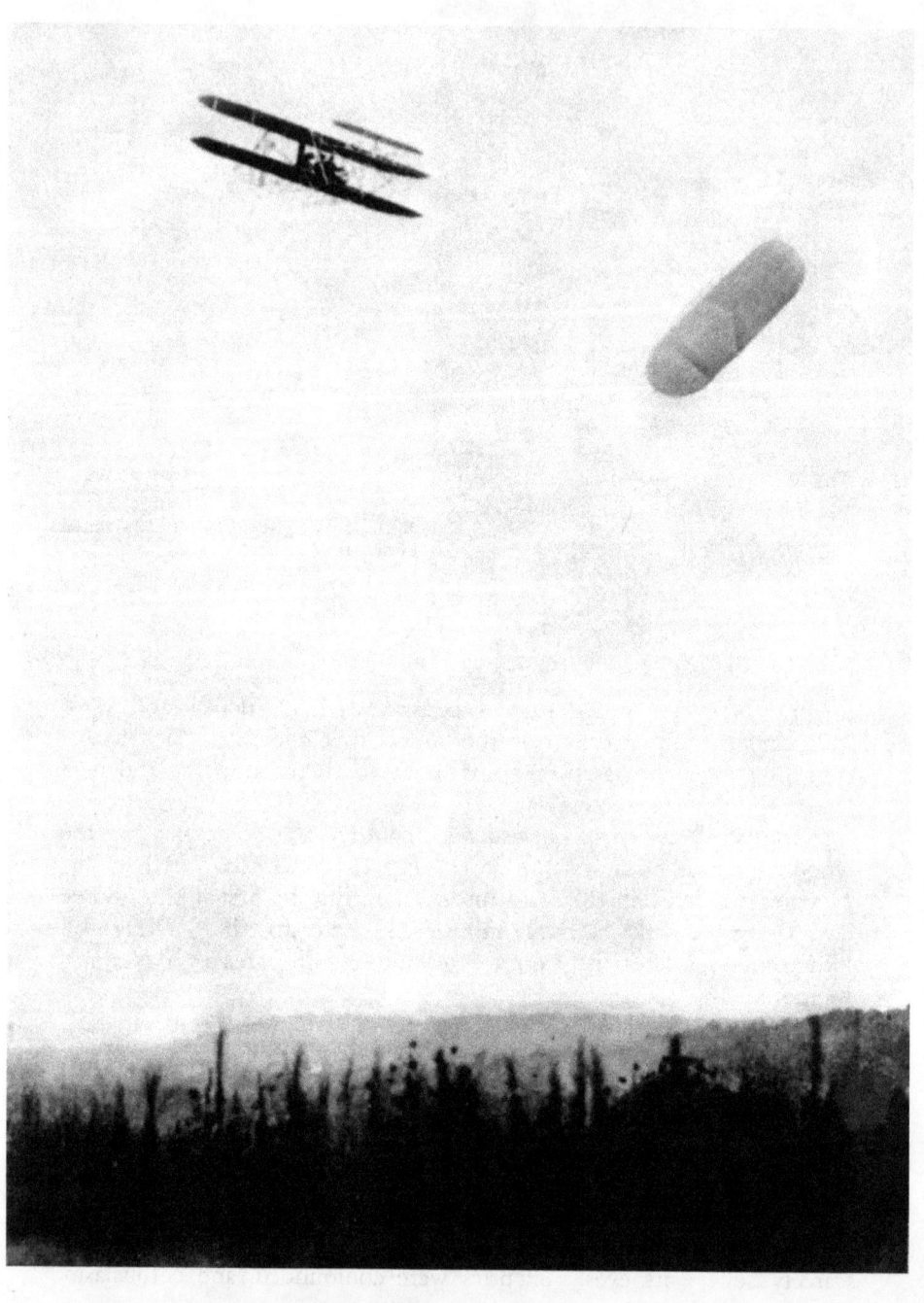

Orville and his passenger, Lt. Benjamin D. Foulois, round the captive balloon which marked the turning point of the Army speed test flight from Fort Meyer, July 30, 1909. The flight was just under 43 miles an hour. *Courtesy, Smithsonian Institution.*

called him a bluffer. The *Figaro* commented, "It was not merely a success but a triumph; a conclusive trial and a decisive victory for aviation, the news of which will revolutionize scientific circles throughout the world." It was a statement to the press by a witness, Maj. B. F. S. Baden-Powell, president of the Aeronautical Society of Great Britain, that is most often quoted: "That Wilbur Wright is in possession of a power which controls the fate of nations is beyond dispute." One of Wilbur's sayings in France became famous: "I know of only one bird, the parrot, that talks," he said, "and it can't fly very high."

Orville's first public flight was on September 3, 1908 at Fort Myer. He circled the field one and one-half times on the first test. "When the plane first rose," Theodore Roosevelt, Jr., recorded "the crowd's gasp of astonishment was not alone at the wonder of it, but because it was so unexpected." Orville's final flight at Fort Myer in 1908 ended in tragedy. The airplane crashed, killing Lt. Thomas Selfridge, a passenger flying with Orville. Orville suffered broken ribs, a fractured leg, and hip injuries.

In 1909, Orville completed the Government test flights by flying 10 miles in 14 minutes, or just under 43 miles an hour. The United States Army formally accepted its first airplane from the Wrights on August 2, 1909. During the same year both brothers made further flying triumphs in Europe where they became famous flying in France and Italy. While Orville was making sensational flights in Germany (as required for the formation of a Wright company in that country), Wilbur, in America, made spectacular flights at New York City where more than a million New Yorkers got their first glimpse of an airplane in the air.

Commercial companies were formed in France and Germany to manufacture Wright planes before the Wright Company was organized in the United States with Wilbur as president and Orville vice president. In financial affairs the Wrights were remarkably shrewd— a match for American and European businessmen. They grew wealthy as well as famous, but they were not happy as businessmen and looked forward to the time when they could retire to devote themselves again to scientific research.

Orville returned to Kill Devil Hills in October 1911 to experiment with an automatic control device and to make soaring flights with a glider. The new device was not tested because of the presence of newspapermen at the camp each day. Orville set a new world's soaring record of 9 minutes and 45 seconds on October 24. This remained the world's record until it was exceeded 10 years later in Germany. On May 30, 1912, Wilbur Wright, aged 45, died of typhoid fever. Orville survived him by 36 years.

The Original Airplane Exhibited

Orville always thought that the National Museum in Washington, administered by the Smithsonian Institution, was the logical place for the original Wright 1903 airplane to be preserved and exhibited. However, for a long time he was unwilling to entrust the airplane there because of a controversy between him and the Smithsonian in regard to the history of the invention of the airplane. In 1928, Orville lent the plane to the Science Museum at South Kensington, near London, England, with the understanding that it would stay there permanently unless he made a written request for its return. Finally, in 1942, the dispute with the Smithsonian was settled to Orville's satisfaction, and the next year he wrote a request to the Science Museum for the return of the airplane to this country when it could be safely shipped after World War II ended.

After Orville Wright's death on January 30, 1948, his executors deposited the original 1903 airplane in the National Air Museum (now the National Air and Space Museum). It was formally placed on exhibition in Washington on December 17, 1948, the 45th anniversary of the first flights. The priceless original airplane now occupies the highest place of honor among other interesting aeronautical exhibits.

The National Memorial

On March 2, 1927, the Congress authorized the establishment of Kill Devil Hills Monument National Memorial to commemorate the Wrights' achievement of the first successful flight of a man-carrying, power-driven, heavier-than-air machine. The area was transferred from the War Department to the National Park Service, U.S. Department of the Interior, on August 10, 1933, and on December 1, 1953, the name was changed to Wright Brothers National Memorial. The memorial contains about 425 acres. It embraces the sites of the first four flights and most of the glider experiments.

Guide to the Area

VISITOR CENTER. The visitor center represents the focal point in the interpretation of the area. In addition to an extensive series of modern museum exhibits telling the story of the memorial, the center also houses an information desk, where literature is available, and the administrative offices of the memorial. From the exhibition rooms, there is a sweeping panoramic view of the reconstructed

Wright brothers' 1903 camp, the first flight grounds where markers designate the take-off and landing points of the first flights, and the Wright memorial shaft atop Kill Devil Hill.

RECONSTRUCTED WRIGHT BROTHERS' 1903 CAMP. About 100 yards southwest of the visitor center stand two wooden structures built by the National Park Service in 1953 on the 50th anniversary of the first flight. They are reconstructions of the Wright brothers' 1903 living quarters and hangar based on historical research and photographs of the originals. The furnishings within the living quarters are of the 1902-3 period, and are almost exact duplications of those used by the Wrights.

FIRST FLIGHT GROUNDS. Less than 100 feet west of the camp is a 10-ton granite memorial boulder placed by the National Aeronautic Association in 1928 on the 25th anniversary of the first flight. The boulder marks the take-off point of the first flight and of the three additional flights made December 17, 1903. A reconstruction of the original single-rail starting track is placed at the north and south sides of the boulder. Four numbered markers north of the boulder designate landing points of the powered flights made on December 17, 1903.

KILL DEVIL HILL. About a quarter of a mile south of the visitor center lies Kill Devil Hill, used by the Wrights for gliding experiments during the period 1900-1903. The north slope of this hill was also used for the unsuccessful attempt at flight on December 14, 1903. Before the Wright memorial shaft was erected, conservation work was begun in 1929 on the massive 26-acre dune of shifting yellow sand to anchor the 91-foot-high dune by seeding it with special grasses adapted to sandy soil.

WRIGHT MEMORIAL SHAFT. Atop Kill Devil Hill stands the striking Wright memorial shaft, a triangular pylon 60 feet high, made of gray granite from Mount Airy, N.C. Construction was begun February 4, 1931, and the shaft was dedicated November 19, 1932. Its sides ornamented with outspread wings in bas-relief, the pylon gives to the eye the impression of a gigantic bird about to take off into space. Stairs lead to the top of the shaft and an observation platform which offers a good view of the surrounding country—magnificent dunes, the Atlantic Ocean, Albemarle Sound, and even West Hill, a quarter of a mile west of the shaft, in the direction of the sound. West Hill, the sand dune which was the scene of many of the Wrights' gliding experiments in 1901-3, was stabilized by the National Park Service in 1934 to preserve the historic site.

Aircraft over the Wright memorial shaft.

Administration

Wright Brothers National Memorial is administered by the National Park Service, U.S. Department of the Interior. A superintendent, whose address is Cape Hatteras National Seashore, Rt. 1, Box 675, Manteo, NC 27954, is in immediate charge.

Glossary

Aileron—A control surface set into or near the trailing edge of an airplane wing, extending, when in the wing, toward the tip and usually within the contour of the wing, and used to control the longitudinal axis of an airplane.

Airborne—Of an airplane or other winged craft: Supported entirely by aerodynamic forces; flying.

Airfoil—A surface or body, as a wing, propeller blade, rudder, or the like, especially designed to obtain a reaction, as lift or thrust, from the air through which it moves.

Angle of attack—The acute angle between the chord of an airfoil, and a line representing the undisturbed relative airflow. Any other acute angle between two reference lines designating the cant of an airfoil relative to oncoming air.

Aspect ratio—The ratio between the span of an airfoil and its chord.

Camber—The curve of an airfoil section from the leading edge to the trailing edge. Camber is usually expressed as the distance from the chord line to the upper or lower surface of an airfoil.

Center-of-pressure travel—The movement, or the amount of movement, of the center of pressure along a chord of an airfoil as the latter is inclined through its normal angles of attack.

Chord—An assumed straight-line tangent to the lower surface of an airfoil section at two points, or a straight line between the leading and trailing edges of an airfoil section, or between the ends of the mean line of an airfoil section; the distance between the leading and trailing edges of an airfoil section.

Drag—A resistant force exerted in a direction opposite to the direction of motion and parallel to the relative gas or air stream.

Dynamic lift—The lift given an airplane by the aerodynamic force produced from an adequately designed airfoil.

Glider—A fixed-wing aircraft having no power plant and constructed so as to glide and soar.

Gliding—The art, science, and activity of moving through the air in a glider.

Heavier-than-air aircraft—Any aircraft weighing more than the air it displaces.

Lift—That component of the total aerodynamic forces acting on an airfoil or on an entire aircraft or winged missile, perpendicular to the relative wind, and exerted, normally, in an upward direction opposing the pull of gravity.

Lighter-than-air aircraft—An aircraft that rises and is supported in air by virtue of a contained gas weighing less than the air displaced by the gas.

Nose dive—A steep dive by, or in, an aircraft.

Power plant—The complete engine or engines in an aircraft, together with propeller or propellers (if any), accessories, fuel and oil tanks and lines, etc.

Powered aircraft—An aircraft having one or more engines, as distinguished from a glider.

Tailspin—A spin, so named in reference to the characteristic spiral action of the tail when the airplane is in a spin.

Warp—To change the shape of something, especially an airplane's wing, by twisting. To give lift or drop to a wing by twisting it at the ends.

Wind tunnel—A chamber through which air is forced at controlled velocities, up to several thousand miles an hour, and in which airfoils, airplanes, missiles, scale models of airplanes, or other objects are mounted in order to observe and study the airflow about such objects, as well as the aerodynamic effects upon them.

Wingspan—The span of a wing, measured or taken between the tips or outermost extremities of either a single-piece wing or a wing that is separated by other aircraft components.

Wing-warping—The action of warping a wing, or a control system for warping the wings at will.

Yaw—An angular displacement or motion to the left or right about the vertical axis of an airplane.

Suggestions for Further Reading

GIBBS-SMITH, C. H., *A History of Flying*. Frederick A. Praeger, New York, 1954.

KELLY, FRED C. (Ed.), *Miracle at Kitty Hawk, the Letters of Wilbur and Orville Wright*. Farrar, Straus and Young, New York 1951.

KELLY, FRED C., *The Wright Brothers*. (A Biography Authorized by Orville Wright.) Harcourt, Brace and Company, New York, 1943.

MCFARLAND, MARVIN W. (Ed.), *The Papers of Wilbur and Orville Wright, including the Chanute-Wright Letters and other Papers of Octave Chanute*. 2 vols., McGraw-Hill Book Company, New York, 1953.

www.ingramcontent.com/pod-product-compliance
Lightning Source LLC
Chambersburg PA
CBHW031421040426
42444CB00005B/672